MAC AND LIL' BIRD

BY STAFFORD L. BOLTON

ILLUSTRATED BY:
ISABELLA ROSS UNREIN

all my love
Mac

BROUGHT TO YOU BY
SUMINSKI FAMILY BOOKS

SPECIAL THANKS TO :

THE BOLTON FAMILY

MAC'S WIFE - **LILLIAN C. BOLTON:** PICTURES OF MAC AND LIL'BIRD

MAC'S DAUGHTERS- **BEVERLY B. DUDLEY:** CONTENT

SUSAN BOLTON AYRES: RECIPES

MAC'S GRANDAUGHTERS- **ALLISON A. MILAM:** TYPED THE ORIGINAL MANUSCRIPT

TRACEY D. WALLS: LEARNING WITH MAC AND FINAL PROOF

MAC'S GREAT GRANDCHILDREN- **EMERSON WALLS:** HOW TO DRAW A CROW

ELIJAH WALLS: CROW FACTS

SUMINSKI FAMILY BOOKS

CLAIRE SUMINSKI: PROJECT MANAGER, EDITING, MARKETING

SUSAN SWEDLUND: LAYOUT, GRAPHIC DESIGN, GAMES

ISABELLA ROSS UNREIN: ILLUSTRATIONS

ANYA UNREIN, HENRIETTA HAITHCOCK AND KELLI KURCZEWSKI- MANUSCRIPT HELP

First Edition
ISBN 979-8-9856781-9-2

Published by Suminski Family Books

suminskifamilybooks.com

TABLE OF CONTENTS

Lil' Bird

INTRODUCTION
BY BEV BOLTON DUDLEY

The mailman assigned to Moss Side Avenue in Richmond, VA, walked briskly up the steps to drop the mail in the slot on our front door. He was surprised to be greeted by a puppy and its companion who were sunning themselves on the porch. He continued down the steps to the next house, but returned a moment later and rang the doorbell. When my mother opened the door, the mailman said, "Lady, did you know there's a pig on your porch?" "Oh, yes, that's Sam," she replied. Baffled, he continued on his route, but turned around and looked back at Sam several times to make sure he really saw a pig, all the while wondering, "Who are these people who have a pig inside the city limits?"

Daddy rescued Sam as a piglet while visiting his mother's farm in North Carolina. Sam's mother had rejected him, so Daddy jumped into the pen and scooped up the squealing piglet. Barely outrunning the angry mama hog, he cleared the fence with one hand, while cradling Sam in the other. My sister, who witnessed the rescue, is still amazed at his athletic ability.

It's an honor to introduce readers to my dad, Stafford L. Bolton (Mac). After high school, he attended North Carolina College of Agriculture and Mechanic Arts (now NC State University) in the school of architecture, but left after four years to join the Army Air Corps as a fighter pilot. It took him four attempts to earn his acceptance to flight school, but he refused to quit. He would not be denied the opportunity to serve his country. He flew strafing missions in the Pacific during World War II, and later became a flight instructor. He referred to himself as "one among many." After the war, he was assigned to the Pentagon, but when he and mother started a family, they relocated to Richmond, VA.

Family life was full of activity and always included lots of animals. During my childhood, we had the usual cats and dogs, but also hamsters, squirrels, chicks, ducks, rabbits, a rooster, a chipmunk, snakes, a fawn, and, of course, Sam. Daddy took his role as head of our household seriously and we respected him. Almost all communication with Daddy went through our mother, but when he spoke, we listened. It was important to him that we develop spiritually, so we never missed a Sunday church service or other church activities. He was a man of his word and was our example of honesty and integrity. When making decisions, he encouraged me to "give it prayerful consideration" and to "just do the right thing."

Sam's rescue – and subsequent residence at 3717 Moss Side Avenue – is a snapshot into my dad's love of animals. So it's no surprise that when the chance to adopt a baby crow presented itself, he seized the opportunity.

"Few have been so privileged and how grateful I am...to share close-up, for five months, the life of one of God's creatures. It was not my purpose to write anything. I only wanted to try and preserve in a very simple way, our unique experience having "Lil Bird" as part of our lives."

Beverly Bolton Dudley
(Mac's Daughter)

"the old man and his crow"

1.

"Few have been so privileged and how grateful I am...to share close-up, for five months, the life of one of God's creatures." Love, Mac

CHAPTER ONE

MY CROW FASCINATION

Dear Reader,
I was born Stafford L. Bolton, but everyone calls me, Mac. This book tells the story of an amazing little crow that came into my life.

Lil' Bird

***What had Mac heard about crows?**

Upon returning home from an early morning Brotherhood Breakfast meeting at the church, my wife Lillian, told me she had seen a small crow in the backyard of the house next door. Thus begins the story of Lil' Bird, the amazing little crow that came into my life. But, I am getting ahead of myself!

My interest in birds and animals went back to the early years of my life. I grew up in a small rural community, Rich Square, in eastern North Carolina during the depression years. Those years were tough. Many people, our family included, depended on wild game, birds, and fish to survive. Hunting and fishing was a way of life in those difficult days, and it provided an important necessity, food for the table. However, my hunting days have long since passed. It is impossible now for me to engage in this activity, even knowing that the herd size of certain animals must be controlled. I leave the hunting for someone else to do.

Over the years I had often heard that crows made interesting pets if adopted when very young. It was said they could be taught to talk by imitating the human voice. Many years ago, during my travels, I had occasion to see one that was tame but did not talk. One person spoke of a crow who could say "school bus" and would announce its approach each day as it came to pick up the children. Another I was told was taught thirty words and would on occasion repeat each one after the other. These stories and others fascinated me. I wanted my own bird in order to discover what these creatures could do. But, I had not the faintest idea how to begin this new adventure.

1

LEARNING WITH MAC: GUIDED QUESTIONS

*What were some of the jobs in the crow family?

***What is the incubation period
for crow eggs?**

Lillian and I loved to watch the crows nesting in our neighbor's yard. We had watched, through field glasses, in the early spring as these birds, a family unit no doubt, built their nest in the very top-most point in a pine tree, which was sixty to seventy feet high.

This we could see from a vantage point inside our kitchen, sighting through a window directly in line with the top of the tree. Field glasses were a great help as we could bring the scene close and observe the activity of the birds. We watched as they worked together building and preparing their nest for the young ones that were to come in the early spring.

They were truly a family group; their movements were planned and they were protective of their young. They drove away all intruders with piercing screeches. Those in and around the nest would fly in circles, ever widening their flight patterns, discouraging again with loud high pitched sounds all intruders in the air or on the ground. If a cat wandered into the area, they would immediately sound the alarm. Their flight patterns would change to a lower level and they would follow the cat as it made its way along the ground and until it had passed through their "territory". We learned early on they did not like nor did they trust cats. Dogs did not seem to bother or make them uneasy. Their nests were easy prey to hawks, especially the young, and we concluded that was the reason the young were never left alone. There were always adults near the nest and on guard.

We knew the laying and later the hatching process was taking place as we could see the nest was now occupied and "mother-bird" was sitting on the eggs. The eggs were not visible to us even with the field glasses, though it was evident as little ones did appear in time, following a twenty-eight day incubation period.

In due time the eggs were hatched and the young appeared in the nest. Again, we observed from time to time how the crow family fed and cared for their young. It appeared this family was made up of about ten adults, each having some specific job to do with the caring for the young. Some brought in food, others cared for the nest and some guarded the surrounding area, sounding an alarm when there was imminent danger.

But, how was I to adopt a young crow? Well, my friend, Reverend Chris Haig, who was a Scottish preacher on Sabbatical, came for a visit. Jokingly, I called his attention to our nesting family of crows in our neighbor's yard and suggested that, since I was 75 and he was younger, he climb the tall pine tree and retrieve one of the little crows from the nest, return it safely to ground level and together we could commence to raise and train it.

Even as I pleaded for his help and let him know just how much I wanted a little crow, he turned a deaf ear to my proposal. Finally, after much prodding, his answer came, "From this vantage point on the ground I somehow do not picture myself – a man of the cloth – engaging in this questionable and dangerous activity!" He concluded that a sane and sensible person would not dare make such stupid suggestions. I must confess my real purpose in all of this was to hear him talk. His Scottish accent fascinated me, especially if he was a little excited as he spoke!

Little did I realize that about four weeks after my Scottish friend returned home, my dream would become reality. Opportunity was about to knock at my door.

LET'S DRAW A CROW!

Follow the steps below to draw a crow. You will need a piece of paper and a pencil. The red line shows what you should draw and the black line shows what you have already drawn.

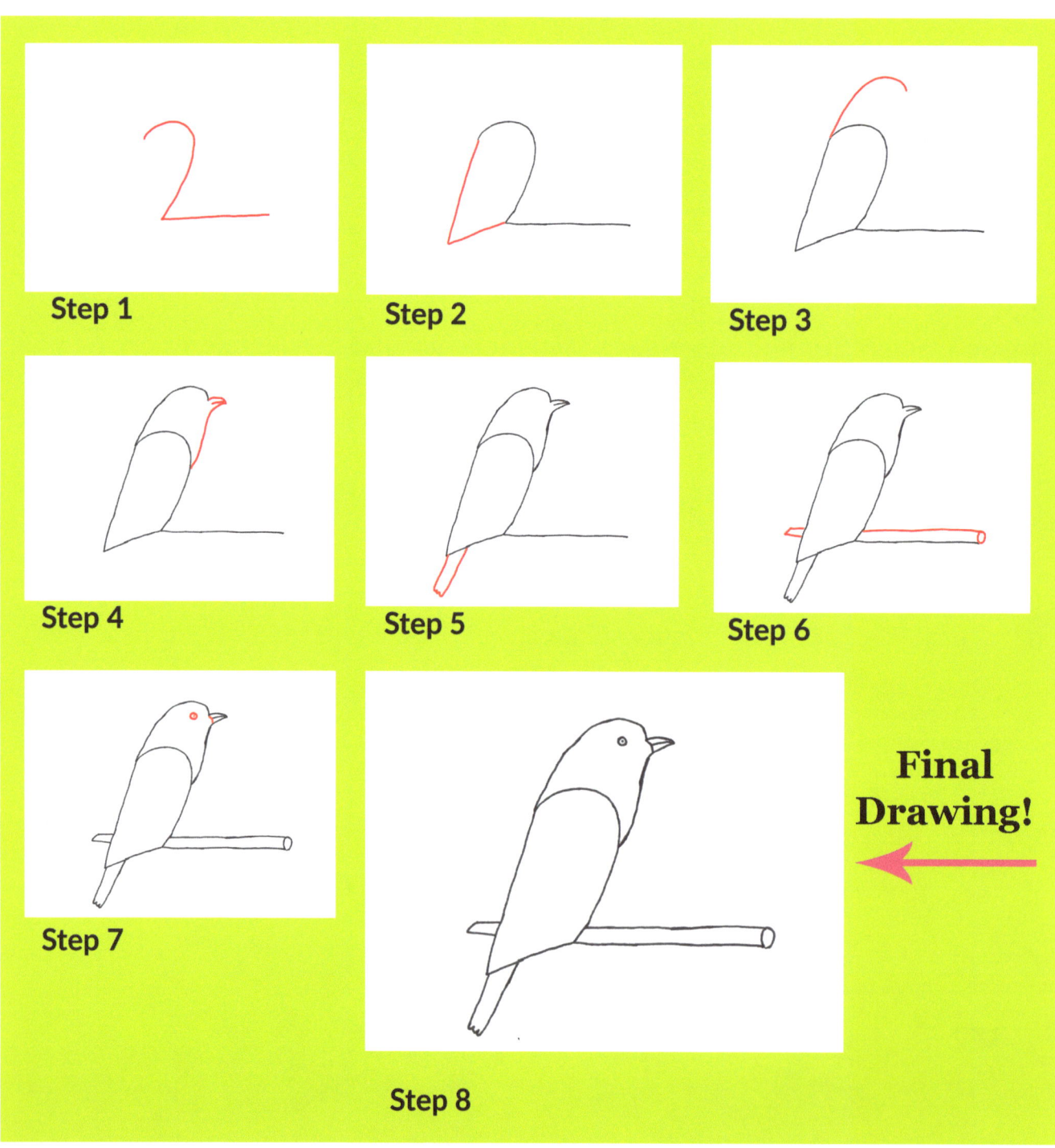

Step 1

Step 2

Step 3

Step 4

Step 5

Step 6

Step 7

Final Drawing!

Step 8

CHAPTER THREE

OPPORTUNITY KNOCKS

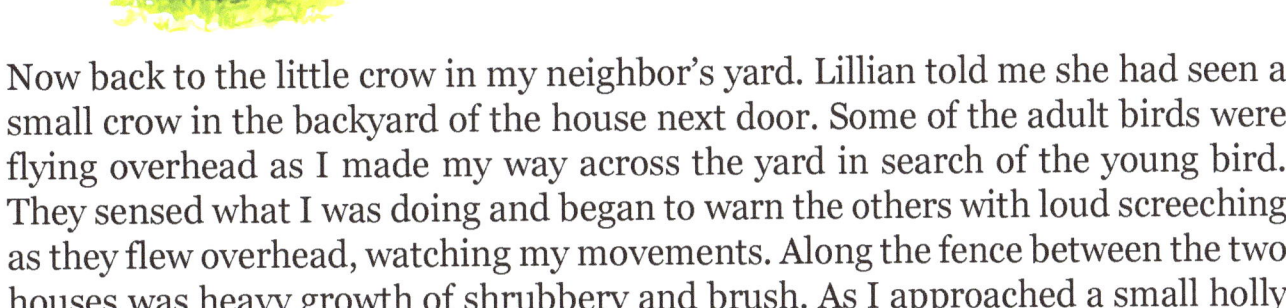

*How did the adult crows react to Mac approaching Lil' Bird?

*How did Lil' Bird react to Mac trying to pick her up?

Now back to the little crow in my neighbor's yard. Lillian told me she had seen a small crow in the backyard of the house next door. Some of the adult birds were flying overhead as I made my way across the yard in search of the young bird. They sensed what I was doing and began to warn the others with loud screeching as they flew overhead, watching my movements. Along the fence between the two houses was heavy growth of shrubbery and brush. As I approached a small holly tree, I could see the little crow sitting calmly on one of the lower branches.

This little bird did not seem frightened by my presence. I moved somewhat closer and reached down to pick it up. I could see it was small but fully feathered and I wondered almost immediately why it was not able to fly. Could it be hurt or injured in some way? I did not want to cause further injury, so I planned to be careful in my effort to rescue it.

When I did reach down to pick it up, it jumped down on the ground and started to run from me. It ran only a short distance and then stopped, turned, looked at me and did not make any further effort to get away. It was as if this little crow was saying, "Please take me with you, I am frightened and need your help." This little bird was on the small side, and we thought it most likely that she was a female. She measured about six to eight inches from the end of her beak to the tip of her tail with a wingspan of maybe ten to twelve inches and was fully feathered. At maturity these birds are up to eighteen inches long and have a wingspan of twenty-four to twenty-eight inches. The males are larger than the females and they weigh between one to one and one-half pounds when fully matured.

She was small and not able to fly. She needed us. Almost in an instant I knew there was going to be a strong bond of friendship between us. I cannot describe how, but I knew it was there.

Did you know?

Crows are from the bird family of Corvids, which are among the smartest animals in the world.

Since the Migratory Bird Act was instated, a license is needed to raise a crow as a pet.

LEARNING WITH MAC: GUIDED QUESTIONS

*Why were Lil' Bird's wings clipped?

*What was Lil' Bird's preferred food?

Not once did she resist me. She very calmly accepted me as I brought her into our house to inspect her for injuries or some other unseen defect. None could be found, so we declared her in good shape. I still could not understand why she could not fly because everything about her told me she was alright.

But her wing and tail feathers, upon examination, seemed uneven, so we clipped them slightly. We learned later this was not the thing to do. We felt we might care for her better if she did not fly until she had gotten older and larger. Anyway, the clipping did not seem to bother her. She rarely attempted to fly. She was quite content just walking around.

Her first home was a large plastic laundry basket turned upside down, much like an old chicken coop. It was late spring 1992 and the days and nights were warm. During the days she was outside in her "coop" with plenty of food and water. At night I moved her inside the garage, placed newspaper on the floor for protection and covered her with her "coop". Surprisingly she seemed to really like her newfound home and was content with her surroundings.

We discovered by trial and error that she would eat almost anything, but she preferred corn meal dampened and rolled in small balls and white bread broken in small pieces soaked in water. Once in a while we did give her small pieces of cooked meat, like hamburger, which she seemed to enjoy.

7

I started working with her by just sitting beside her "coop" in a chair and talking to her. I would repeat the word "hello" over and over again and would hold my hand near so she could see it. After about three or four days I would slip my hand inside her "coop" and try to touch her. After several days she allowed me to touch her and even stroke her back a little. What I really wanted her to do was stand on my hand, but at first, she would not do this.

A few more days passed and my wife, Lillian, and I decided we needed to get her out of her "coop". She probably would do better with more freedom of movement on the ground. The question was how this could be done without any danger to her. I did not want her to get hurt in any way.

Finally, we decided to use a five foot lead attached to her leg. With Lillian holding her, I was able to put a small plastic ring around each leg. They were loose fitting so the lead could be snapped onto either of the plastic rings.

The little crow took this like a duck to water. When I put her down on the ground, she walked around with me holding on, as if this had been her way of life all along. She did not mind it at all. We would walk in the yard and up and down the sidewalks. We both enjoyed these walks together.

Did you know?

Crows are a type of songbirds. They have many different calls that communicate information to other crows. They also can mimic human speech.

Crow Calls : companion call, air excitement, danger call, assembly call, predatory alarm (cat), female call, male call, juvenile call, baby begging and feeding sounds, and the "I've got food!" call.

https://www.youtube.com/watch?v=s1gxWM_E_D8

CHAPTER FIVE — LEARNING NEW TRICKS

*How did Lil' Bird let people know if they had gotten too close to her?

*How did Lil' Bird show Mac that she was listening when he spoke to her?

*What kinds of things did Lil' Bird like to play with?

People passing by were amazed by her actions and how completely satisfied she seemed to be performing this way – and a performer she was! She did not mind showing off but she did not want anyone to get too close. She had her way of letting you know not to get too near. She would open her mouth and the noise that came out could not have been confused with any other message, "Don't come any closer, I don't like it". You could almost sense this was what she was saying.

She learned very quickly to get on my arm. I could tell when she was tired of walking and I would offer my arm down low and she would jump on for me to carry her, which I did. All the while we were together I talked to her reminding her time and again of the word "hello". She did not respond at first.

We spent many hours sitting on our front porch, rocking in the chair. Most of the time she would be on my arm or maybe sitting on the back of the chair pulling my hair, grabbing the lobs of my ears and pulling. She did not hurt me. Nor did she try.

Her bite was very gentle, and she seldom used her bill or beak to peck. In any case, she was harmless. If I needed to get up and leave a few minutes, I would tie the lead to the chair and go. When I returned, she would be where I had left her. She seemed to know what she was supposed to do. I would never leave her alone for very long because of the danger of cats in the area. She was very helpless since she could not fly and had no way of defending herself. Her only defense was to fly out of harm's way. This she could not do.

10

There is a large oak tree in our backyard that shades a large area. On the hottest days, it is refreshing and comfortable sitting and relaxing under the shelter of its branches. We spent much time doing just that. She on my arm, me in a chair, and just maybe she would be walking on the ground, around the chair. The five-foot lead allowed her a great deal of freedom to do this. She seemed to want to be near me. I continued to talk to her and noticed that she was watching me as I spoke.

She would cock her head sideways and look directly at me very intently trying to take in what I was saying. I began to reach down to have her jump on my arm and would bring her very close to speak to her. She always obliged me when I asked for cooperation.

Not a day passed that I was not with her three to four hours. I know this all paid off, as the results will bear this out. She was extremely easy to work with and seemed anxious to please me and make me proud of her accomplishments.

She was never wild. It was as if she was tame right from the start. The only things that seemed to bother her were sudden noises, like gun fire, or the approach of a stranger. Her instinct was to get out of the way and to find a place to hide. She could not do this, of course, because I was holding on to the lead. Even her fears would pass quickly, and she would calm down after I talked with her for a bit.

She had a very keen sense of hearing and her ability to see amazed me. She would see and retrieve any little object that was shiny or reflected light. This little crow would then proceed to hide it, covering it with grass, leaves, small branches or anything she could find. Days later she would retrieve it, play with it for a while and then hide it again.

CHAPTER SIX

OUR DAILY ROUTINE

LEARNING WITH MAC: GUIDED QUESTIONS

*How did Lil' Bird greet Mac in the mornings?

*When Mac became concerned about
Lil' Bird's "quarters" in the garage,
where did he move her?

We made a new home for her in our garage because she had outgrown the plastic "coop" and needed more space. I laid some plastic sheeting on the floor and placed an old cedar fence post on the plastic as her perch. I would tie the lead to the post so she could not wander off the plastic floor protector. When I introduced her to this arrangement, she seemed to know exactly what it was for. In the late evenings, when roosting time was near, she would lead me to her night-time home, where she would take her position on her roost and there she would stay. She always had plenty of food and water nearby.

When I went to let her out in the morning, she would greet me by gently flapping her wings. She did this in the same manner that young birds do when adult birds approach. At feeding time she would jump on my arm and we would visit for a minute. Then I would take her into our kitchen and help her to perch on the back of a chair. As we ate our breakfast, I would offer her bits of bread, small pieces of meat and water out of a glass. Later she would learn to drink Pepsi-Cola from a glass.

She tolerated Lillian, but would not accept any food from her hand. She would back away and let Lillian know by the noise she made, not to bother her. I was the only one who could hold or touch her. She did not mind if I stroked her back, rubbed her head or touched her breast. Sometimes I would hold her beak closed with my hand. She did not take kindly to that and would in no uncertain terms tell me so.

I began to be concerned about her "quarters" in the garage and decided a change was in order. I wanted her near so I could easily check on her at night. I worried, too, about the possibility of a cat or some other animal getting into the garage. The garage was very secure, but I was still concerned, so I moved her to the basement of our home.

The new arrangement was much better. She did not mind, and we felt safety was now on our side. I could check on her anytime day or night. If the weather outside was unfavorable, we could be together and our "training" could continue uninterrupted. By this time, she had learned to make a noise, which I soon learned was her calling me to come. She would continue this flapping of her wings to acknowledge my approach. It was as if she was saying, "You need to pay more attention to me! I want to play!" or asking, "Where have you been?" She always greeted me this way and later she extended this same courtesy to Lillian. At the end of the day, I would tie the lead to her post, place food and water nearby and bid her goodbye. The light would be turned off; she would have already positioned herself on her roost, and would remain in that spot throughout the night. I never went to bed without checking on her first. I made sure her lead was not tangled and that she had freedom of movement. We heard nothing from her until the next morning. Thirty or forty minutes after day light she would "sound-off" her familiar call for us to come and feed her.

We made haste in responding mainly to reduce the volume of noise. I would be greeted by the flapping of her wings and the noise would stop. Before I could untie her lead, she was on my arm ready to go. If I did not work fast enough, she would get on my back or shoulder which made it more difficult to get the lead untied.

We headed straight for the kitchen, where she would perch on the back of one of the kitchen chairs. She was ready to eat! We had a special dish for her, sitting atop a stack of telephone directories. This brought the food to her level. She would eat her breakfast with us; pieces of bread soaked in water, corn meal balls, scrambled eggs and most of the things that we ate. She was not picky as far as food was concerned. If she saw something on your plate that she liked, she would try to get it.

She grew steadily and became stronger; however, her feathers did not seem to grow in the same proportion as her body. We decided this was because we had clipped her feathers. After about three weeks in the basement, we thought she might need to be outside in the open. She would require protection and shelter from the elements and from predators.

CHAPTER SEVEN

HELLO, LIL' BIRD!

LEARNING WITH MAC: GUIDED QUESTIONS

*Why did Lil' Bird pretend to have a broken wing?

*Did Lil' Bird ever sit on Lillian's arm?

Lillian suggested that we give our young crow a name. Up to this point we had not called her by any name, although we continued to greet her often with the word "hello". So far there had been no response. She seemed to listen to what was being said, but no answer came. Our feeling now was that adding another word or two in greeting her, might spark a response. So, after a process of elimination we settled on "Lil' Bird" as her name. From that moment on we always called her by name and said "hello" when in her presence.

She picked up on this very quickly. Almost from the beginning Lil' Bird recognized her name. She would come to me when I called her from then on. Even if she was playing around my feet on the ground and I called her name she would look at me, head cocked sideways as if to say, "Yes, I do know my name!"

Lillian continued to get Lil' Bird to be more friendly with her by gradually moving closer and closer to her. She would talk to her and reach out with her hand at the same time to try and reassure her of Lillian's friendly intent. After some considerable time, she managed to get her hand within inches of touching the little crow. However, upon trying to further close the gap, Lil'Bird would give Lillian the broken wing treatment.

Both male and female crows do this to lead predators away from the young birds. They also do this to signal their little ones to seek cover from danger. Lil' Bird was good at this trick.

As soon as Lillian's hand got within eight or ten inches of touching her, her wing would go down and touch the ground. She would then start walking in a circle, dragging her wing on the ground and of course, sounding-off in her noisy way. This was a signal not to get any closer and to leave her alone!

It did seem rather strange that she would do this even though there were no young ones present. Our conclusion was she did this out of instinct to protect herself and her territory. I found it quite amusing to watch her perform in this way if Lillian tried to get too close.

Only on one or two rare occasions was Lillian able to get her to sit on her arm. If I was away for a long time and Lillian was bird-sitting and needed to be in her house, Lil' Bird would very reluctantly accept a free-ride. However, she would "complain" all the way to her destination. To her this arrangement was most unsatisfactory. Even in this situation she would not let Lillian touch her, she was only glad to get Lil' Bird safely in her house and get the door closed.

So we needed to get Lil' Bird out of her basement surroundings into open country. She needed a place of her own. Protection from predators and the elements were of primary concern. Our neighborhood had plenty of cats roaming in the area.

Did you know?

Crows often use tools to get food. For example, they will use sticks to get ants out of their nests and knock plums out of trees. They also put nuts in the road, wait for a car to run them over, and then swoop in to gather the nuts out of the cracked shells.

CHAPTER EIGHT

LIL' BIRD GETS A NEW HOME

*What did Lil' Bird do if another bird got into her new house?

*What part of Lil' Bird's body was not growing with the rest of her?
Why was this a problem?

We settled on a plan to build a house four by eight feet, with one half of the house being about six feet tall. There would be a simple slant roof, with plastic corrugated material for covering. The upper section of the six-foot part would be enclosed with the same corrugated material. The remaining part with one inch chicken mesh wire. A full-length screen door would then provide complete enclosure. The roosting bars were placed at different levels, with the topmost bar being out of reach of the wind and rain. We then connected all of these levels with a small ladder, so Lil' Bird could make her way from ground level to the top by climbing the ladder. She could then return to the ground by jumping from bar to bar.

Lil' Bird really amazed me when I introduced her to her new quarters. I had to place her inside for the first time. After that, she would go on her own or I might entice her at feeding time. She had not been inside one minute when she spotted the ladder. After a minute or two of careful examination, I watched her go from bottom to top as if she had done this many times before. Just as if to ask, "What else do you want me to do?" She loved her home and did not like intruders.

We had a bird feeder nearby and this attracted other birds and pigeons. Sometimes a bird or pigeon would get inside her place. It made no difference how far away she was when she saw it, she would make a bee line for her house and drive them right out. She did not want to share her place with any other feathered friends.

One day Lillian was called upon to rescue a small sparrow who had unwittingly gotten inside of Lil' Bird's house. As she watched from the porch, there seemed to be a disturbance happening. Lil' Bird caught a sparrow inside of her place and wanted this other bird out. She immediately went inside and began to attack the smaller bird. Using her wings and beak she finally cornered it and if Lillian had not taken immediate action, the small bird would not have made it. Lillian went inside Lil' Bird's house and calmed her. She picked up the slightly wounded sparrow and held it long enough for the bird to gather its senses. Then it flew away. Lil' Bird did not allow other birds in her place. She did not appreciate the company. She was very private, and did not appreciate her privacy being invaded.

Lil' Bird quickly adjusted to the out-of-doors and to all of the surroundings. Her growth was noticeable, especially her body, however, her feathers, wings and tail, were not showing very much progress.

I tried to remember back some several years to my younger days in the country. My mother used to trim the chicken wings to keep them at home and in the yard. I can recall even now helping her do this but had no recollection as to how long it took before the chickens were flying again. I knew it had to be repeated at intervals.

Now I began to wonder if Lil' Bird would ever fly, if she would get new feathers or if the ones we cut would finally grow out again. I was quite concerned! I watched other crows fly overhead, and could see their wider wing spans and larger tails. It was not hard to figure out that Lil' Bird was in deep trouble and that I was the one responsible. I worried about her and was very careful not to leave her alone, unattended outside of her house.

Did you know?

A crow's diet consists of insects, bird eggs, corn and other grains, fish, fruit, nuts and seeds. They are scavengers, so they will eat most anything. They often hide their food under leaves to protect it from other animals.

LEARNING WITH MAC: GUIDED QUESTIONS

*What would Lil' Bird do to Mac's clothing?

*What makes crows so clumsy when they walk?

*Describe Lil' Bird's behavior when she was trying to talk to Mac.

For the next four or five weeks we were together for hours upon hours. I kept the lead on her leg, but by now I allowed her to drag it. I did not always hold on to it. We sat beneath the big oak tree in the back yard. It was a cool and refreshing place to relax. Lil' Bird sat on my arm, in my lap and on my foot. Her favorite place was on my shoulder or the back of the chair. She would try to pull the buttons off my clothes, pull on all the loose threads she could find, and untie my shoes. She took great delight in this. My shoes were seldom tied if she was around. We spent lots of time walking around the yard together, front and back. She seemed to like walking on the sidewalk, which was easier for her.

Crow's feet are quite large for their size. Their feet get in the way, causing them to stumble and sometimes wobble from side to side as if they are drunk. They even fall on the ground quite easily and find it necessary to roll from side to side to get back on their feet. In other words, they are just plain clumsy.

When Lil' Bird was tired of walking, she would get directly in front of me, under my feet and look up. This was the signal for me to pick her up. She often made a soft noise as I reached down for her to get on my arm. Our walks continued and sometimes Lil' Bird would ride on my shoulder.

One day, while talking to her, repeating her name and saying "hello", Lil' Bird started making these guttural and throaty sounds. She looked at me as if to say, "I am ready to talk to you now", and from that time on she sounded-off all the time. She would begin by lowering her head against her breast as if she was getting a deep breath of air and as she slowly raised her head, out would come all these weird sounds. She did this repeatedly. When she stopped, I would follow up with her name and a greeting. As time passed, I felt she was trying to form words and repeat what I was saying. She was trying very hard to accommodate me.

Sometimes she would put her face within an inch or two of mine and make a variety of sounds, as if to ask, "Why can't you understand me?" She was a very persistent lady, and I could not help being impressed with her determination to communicate and work together.

Did you know?

Crows give their owner a name. The name is a unique sound they only use around their owner.

CHAPTER TEN

BATH TIME!

LEARNING WITH MAC: GUIDED QUESTIONS

*How did Lil' Bird feel about her bathtub and bath time?

*How long did it take for Lil' Bird to preen her feathers after bath time?

*What did Mac use to protect his arm from Lil' Bird's claws?

Lil' Bird really did blossom when we released her completely from her lead. She was ready, and I knew she would not go any place, because she still could not fly. While she was still walking around, she learned she could leap or jump with her wings helping her along the way. She was now free to roam the yard, going in and out of her house at her pleasure. We lined the inside of our board fence with one-inch mesh wire, so she would not wander out into the street.

Automobile traffic was very heavy around our house and her fate was in my hands, so I felt it absolutely necessary to do this. It took Lillian and I all day to finish this task and we rested on our pillows well that night, knowing that Lil' Bird could not get out of the yard.

And she never did get out or even try. I do believe she knew what we were trying to do to protect her. Our yard is quite large, which gave her plenty of space to explore and she proceeded to use every inch of it. I placed a large bowl of water in her house to make sure she always had an ample supply of fresh drinking water. One day I noticed she was attempting to take a bath in this bowl. She was standing on the edge and splashing the water with her head and her body and under her wings. She would extend her wings out, so she could get the water in the right place. This of course was an indication to me that she just might like to have a larger container of water for bathing purposes.

I discovered a large plastic pan, about eighteen inches by twenty-four inches and three inches deep, in my garage. I cleaned it up, placed it in the shade of the tree and filled it with water. Mind you now, she was watching all of this, under my feet, wondering, I am sure, what I was doing. She had a lot of curiosity. In a matter of minutes, she was in the middle of the pan of water, hitting the water with her wings and causing the water to fly in all directions. When she got out of the pan, she was soaking wet, feathers dripping water. She loved her new bathtub and used it every day, sometimes two or three times, depending on how hot it was that day.

While she was bathing, I would watch from a nearby chair. She would run over to the chair, since she could not fly, and look at me. This was her way of saying, "Ok, I want you to hold me while I preen my feathers." I would hold my arm down and she would jump on. Then I would place my arm on the chair's armrest, and she would shake herself vigorously, getting me very wet. She would then proceed to dry herself off, preparing each feather very carefully. This would require anywhere from thirty to forty-five minutes, but when she had completed the job, she would be dry and her feathers, beautiful. This was a ritual that took place every day and then some. As she got heavier on my arm, her claws began to dig into my flesh, sometimes almost drawing blood. I used a heavy stocking on my arm, like a sleeve, to get around this. It was more comfortable for her and at the same time made it easier on me. Her intent was not to hurt me, it was just that she was having a hard time keeping her balance and preening feathers at the same time. I tried several times to get her to sit on the arm of the chair, but she would have no part of that. If I put her on the arm of the chair, then placed my arm in some other position she would find a way to get on my arm, no matter what I did. She wanted it her way.

Later I found a deeper pan. It was about four inches deep. Out of curiosity, I decided to see if she would get into the water that deep, because she would almost have to swim to stay in the pan. As soon as I filled it, to my utter surprise she jumped in, proceeded to duck her head under water, beat the water with her wings as before, and get herself soaking wet. She never, to my knowledge, returned to bathe in the smaller pan. She really did enjoy her bathtub. Her antics were fascinating. She never failed to come to me after her bath, expecting me to hold her while she completed her drying time. I moved farther and farther away from her to see if distance made any difference. No matter where I was sitting, she would come running as soon as she had finished.

Bath time was a very special time for Lil' Bird.

Did you know?

Crows show a behavior called "anting" where they rub ants against their feathers. The ants secrete formic acid, which acts as a repellent against parasites and harmful microorganisms.

CHAPTER ELEVEN

CAR RIDE ANYONE?

LEARNING WITH MAC: GUIDED QUESTIONS

*If Lil' Bird noticed Mac going to his car, how did she respond?

*Why did visitors to the Bolton home have to be careful about closing their car doors?

One day, while walking together in the front yard, where our car was parked in the driveway, Lil' Bird hesitated and looked up at the open window. This was a hint to me that she might get into the car if I opened the door. After opening the door, I got in and sat down in the driver's seat. She watched me very carefully and started moving back and forth, looking at me and trying to decide what she should do. Should she get in or not? I continued to talk to her, as I always did, holding my arm as low as I could, hoping she would jump on. After a few minutes of urging, she jumped onto my arm. I brought her inside of the car. She was not the least bit disturbed or frightened by these new surroundings. I then set her down on the back of the passenger seat. She seemed satisfied with this situation, so I decided to start the car and move it back and forth in the driveway, to see if this movement would make her uncomfortable. I did this several times and she sat perfectly still, only moving to hold on as I changed from forward to reverse. I felt at this point that she would be able to ride in a car without any trouble. We rode around the block several times. She moved from her position on the back of the seat to my shoulder, then onto the floor to explore, then back to the seat again. As we rode, she was not afraid of the motion of the car, and watched carefully what was taking place on the outside. I never would have expected this if it was not actually happening to me.

I had a large painter's drop cloth, which I spread inside the car, covering the front and back seats. With this in place, we rode all over the city together. People who passed and saw her sitting with me would do a double-take, not believing what they had seen.

24

When I parked in front of a store, and went inside to purchase something, people would gather around the car to see her. She would always follow me with her eyes, as I would enter and leave the store. She never took her eyes off me. When I would get back to the car, people would say, "That bird knows you, look how she is watching you!" They would always ask what kind of bird it was, which surprised me, because crows are common. I thought everyone knew a crow when they saw one. Then they would want to know why she did not try to get out of the car. I suppose they expected to see a flurry of feathers resulting from a frightened little bird. That never happened; she was always very calm. She never tried to get out of the car, unless I got out stood by the door and called her by name. At times she would not get out, because, for some reason, she enjoyed riding in the car. She still could not fly, so it was jump in and jump out.

Later, when she started flying, it was very fun. She insisted that when the car left the driveway, unless she was in her house with the door closed, she was going to go with me. After she learned to fly, we were not as hesitant to leave her alone. Of course, that meant she might be any place, any time, in a nearby tree, on top of the house or garage, or playing alone in the backyard. If I went out to get into the car to go someplace, and she saw or heard me, in a matter of seconds she would come flying. She would land on the hood of the car and wait for me to open the door, so she could get in. There was no way to get her off the hood, except to open the door and let her in. She was not going to be left behind. Riding in a car was her favorite activity. If she heard the motor start, she lost no time in making her presence known.

On occasion, when the car was in the street, ready to move into traffic, she would come flying. Suddenly, there she would be, sitting on the hood, as if she had appeared out of thin air. Then it was the same routine. Open the door and let her get in and she was happy and ready to go! If friends drove into the yard, they had to be careful to close their car doors or Lil' Bird would make herself at home in their cars, too. Upon returning from an outing, I would get out of the car and stand by the door. Lil' Bird would jump to the ground and follow me up the steps and into the house, just like you might expect a pet dog or cat to do.

If she heard the motor start, she lost no time in making her presence known.

25

CHAPTER TWELVE

SNACK TIME FOR LIL' BIRD

LEARNING WITH MAC: GUIDED QUESTIONS

*How would Lil' Bird eat her cookies and peanut butter crackers?

*Where did Lil' Bird store food?

*What were some of the places that Lil' Bird would try to hide her food?

Lil' Bird would make her way to the kitchen, hop up on a chair and ask for food. By now her favorites were butter cookies and peanut butter on a cracker. She dearly loved both. We kept cookies in a metal container on a shelf in the small butler's pantry, between the dining room and kitchen. She would take her position on the floor and point with her wings to the metal containers. She knew exactly where we kept them. We would hand her a cookie and off she would go to the back porch. There she would shatter the snack with her beak into small pieces and eat it. Later in the day, I would hand Lil' Bird a peanut butter cracker and she would do the same thing again. Usually, she would end up with peanut butter all over her beak. The next time she came near me, I would reach down and wipe her beak clean with my fingers. She allowed me to do this and seemed glad to get the peanut butter off.

Lil' Bird never tried to bite or peck me. I could put my finger in her mouth and when she clamped down, it was very gentle. Occasionally, she would hop up in my lap to eat a butter cookie. To break it up into small pieces, she held it with her foot and hit it hard with her beak. Sometimes she would miss the cookie and hit my leg or arm. I was surprised by how hard she could hit an object or cookie! Believe me, I could feel it! Sometimes she even drew blood. Lil' Bird was never vicious, nor did she intentionally try to harm anyone. She would be described as very gentle and loving.

Along with butter cookies and peanut butter on a cracker she liked hard cat food and cracked corn. I discovered she had what seemed to be a small pouch in her throat. She could and did store food there. Apparently, there was also another storage area, in her digestive system, in which she stored food to later regurgitate.

Did you know?

The crop is like a "doggy bag" when the bird eats. Many birds eat as much as possible when the opportunity for feeding presents itself. This food can't possibly be digested this quickly. The crop enables the bird to fill up and then the bird can do the digesting later when it has time to rest and avoid predators that may be lurking nearby while the bird is in the act of eating. *(There is more information on a bird's digestive system and a game in the back of the book.)*

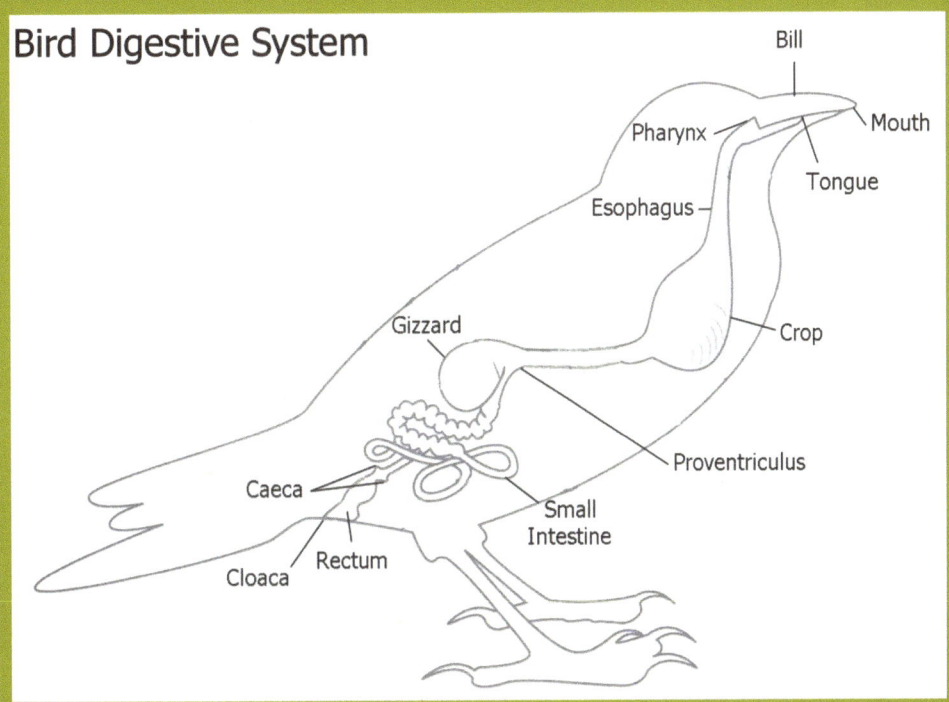

Bird Digestive System

No matter how much food, great or small, was placed in her dish, she never left any behind. She would eat a small amount, then would proceed to hide the rest all over the yard. She would fill her pouch with food and then hide it in crevices, cracks, under leaves, in clumps of grass, under sticks; you name it. She did this day in and day out. Lil' Bird always quickly emptied her dish. Occasionally, I would remove a leaf or sticks with which she had covered her food, and she would immediately pick the item up and hide her food under it again. She tried to put her food in my shoes, in my shirt pocket and even in the creases of my clothes. She was not choosy where she put her food. Twice she found juicy earthworms in the yard, ran over and tried to stuff them in my shoe. I always allowed her to complete her work, when she tried the first time. The second time she tried, I would say, "No!" To get her attention, all that was needed was to carry her food dish. Then, she would follow you anywhere! Lil' Bird was always looking for cookies and peanut butter on a cracker.

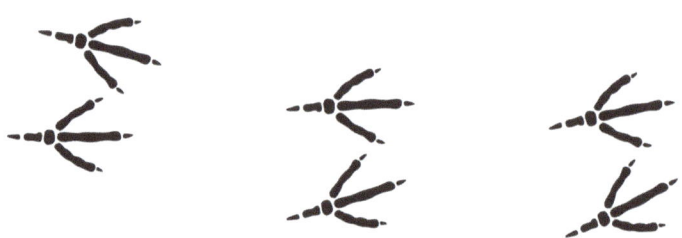

When Lil' Bird completely emptied the food dish, she would turn it upside down. It was interesting how she did this. She would rotate her head 180 degrees, and in so doing, would flip the dish over in a split second, with little or no effort. I did not realize crows had the ability to do this. I was aware owls and other species could do this, but not crows.

Did you know?

Crows are skilled hunters; they wade chest deep into lakes and streams and snatch fish out of the water. They also dig up clams.

CHAPTER THIRTEEN

MORE SKILLS AND ANTICS

LEARNING WITH MAC: GUIDED QUESTIONS

*What did Lil' Bird leave in her food dish for Mac?

*How did Lil' Bird let Mac know she was ready to play?

In building Lil' Bird's house, as most builders do, I dropped nails and wire staples all around the place. I picked up some, but many I missed. For several days after its completion and after it became her home, when I would go to pick up her food dish there would be two or three nails and staples she had found and deposited in the dish. The dish was always upright with the items for me to remove. This continued for several days until there was nothing left for her to return. It was as if she was saying, "I am trying to help you clean up your mess. You should be more careful next time!"

On occasion, it would be necessary for me to be away from the house for several hours. Before she could fly, it was a must to keep a very watchful eye out for Lil' Bird when she was out of her house or wandering around in the yard. Lillian then would become a bird-sitter. She needed to keep Lil' Bird in her sight almost all of the time. From Lillian's vantage point, seated on the porch swing, she could see most of our backyard. Lil' Bird seemed satisfied and content to just wander and explore all parts of the yard; however, danger from cats was always in the back of our minds. Because of this, we maintained an almost constant vigil when she was alone.

I always looked forward to coming home just to see her reaction and what she would do. There seemed to be something different every time. Before she could fly, she would greet me each time with a gentle flapping of her wings, no matter where she was in the yard. This was her way of saying hello.

29

She would then run straight for me, and as I entered the gate she would be at my feet, waiting for me to pick her up. As I offered my arm for her to hop on, she would begin her conversation, all sorts of noises. I knew what she was saying. As she looked directly at me it was as if she was saying, "Why did you leave without me? You know how I love to ride in the car. I wanted to go with you!"

After she began to fly, if she saw me drive into the driveway, I would barely get the engine stopped before she would land on the hood of the car. When I opened the door, she would immediately get inside, perch herself on the back of the seat and look at me as if to say, "Ok let's go, you left me, now you must drive me around for a while. I wanted to ride, too!" And so off we would go for a ride. We would really attract a lot of attention from passersby and from folks in the cars we would meet, especially those waiting at stoplights. Lil' Bird did not look from side to side as she rode, but straight ahead. She needed to bend forward slightly to see out, as she was too tall to have good visibility when upright. She really did look funny the way she positioned herself to see what was going on. Most of the time she just perched herself on the back of the passenger seat very contentedly. I was amazed that Lil' Bird was not the least bit frightened by what was going on around her. I could not help but wonder why she wanted to ride in an automobile. She dearly loved these outings.

Returning, we would find a cool shady spot under the big oak tree. We would sit and talk or just maybe she would have her bath. She would then preen her feathers as I watched. I talked to her, hoping that with my efforts, I could get her to say just one understandable word. Apparently, that was not to be and I was disappointed. However, the other pleasures she so freely gave, more than offset any disappointment I had. Each passing day Lil' Bird presented me with something new. She would try out a new antic, a different look or maybe just a new show of affection.

Never, in my wildest imagination, could I have possibly known what was going to happen to me. How this little creature would take over my life for the five months she was with us. The bonding between us, and our mutual love and respect, was a closeness that only we could understand. I am saddened by this at times, because these memories are not easily forgotten. On the other hand, I am filled with joy and excitement, having been blessed with an experience so few people are privileged to enjoy.

Before Lil' Bird began to fly, I would play with her in the yard, which was like playing with a dog. Her favorite game was playing with a stick or a piece of cloth. I would hold a stick and she would try to snatch it away from me. She was much stronger than you would imagine and would hang on for dear life, even when I would lift her clear off the ground. She would hang on and swing back and forth as if she was holding on to a piece of cloth or rope.

Lil' Bird would let you know she wanted to play by finding her own stick and bringing it to you. When she was ready to stop, she would take the stick away some distance and drop it. Usually after a session like this, she was tired and would then get in my lap for a rest. I would cover her with my coat, and she would snuggle up real close to me, as if trying to hide. Her rest periods were short-lived, and it was not long before she was down on the ground playing around my feet again.

One day she was playing some few feet away and I called her by name to see if she would recognize her name. She looked at me and started to run towards me. Whether she did it on purpose or stumbled accidentally, I do not know, but she did a complete forward "flip" and landed on her feet. Her head went down, and she rolled forward and over, a perfect roll. I have only seen her do this once.

Another day, while sitting in the yard with her, Lil' Bird was running around my chair. After the second lap around, she rolled onto her back and was laying upside down on the ground, with her little feet sticking straight up in the air; looking up at me. My first thought was that she had injured herself in some way and was hurt. But the look in her eyes was different. As if to say, "Well, what do you think of this?"

I still was not sure, and did not touch her at first. She continued to lie there for a few seconds, after which I reached down and flipped her back on her feet. I think that is what she wanted me to do. She was playing with me. I never got tired of her antics!

"I never got tired of her antics!"

CHAPTER FOURTEEN

PIGEONS, SQUIRRELS AND MORE

LEARNING WITH MAC: GUIDED QUESTIONS

*What did Lil' Bird do when the squirrel tried to bump her?

*What mischief did Lil' Bird make when Mac was trying to assemble his new grill?

*What special visitor became friends with Lil' Bird?

For some reason Lil 'Bird did not like pigeons or squirrels, and they worried her to the extent that she did not want either on the ground near her. Our bird feeder attracted both, as they came to pick up the food that had fallen from the feeder onto the ground. She still could not fly, but she drove the pigeons off by running and rushing toward them, as if she was going to attack. And she kept them at bay. She also attacked the squirrels in the same way, except she would run at them and bump against them. This did not last for long because the squirrels did not go for this kind of treatment from a bird! They started giving her the same treatment. They would rush at her and bump up against her. The squirrel's bump was a little more forceful than Lil' Bird's. I wondered how this would all work out. To my amazement, one day Lil' Bird gave the squirrel a good bump and he turned to return the favor. As he made his pass, Lil' Bird jumped straight up and he ran underneath her. He turned to make a second pass, and she did the same thing again. He missed both times, to his dismay! This activity became a game with Lil' Bird. I watched many occasions of repeated instances which she seemed to enjoy. The squirrel might give up and leave for the day, but he would be back later. The squirrels were not able to take advantage of her after she learned this trick! Mind you, all of this would take place within ten or fifteen feet away from me sitting in my chair. The squirrels were quite brazen and did not fear people in the least.

Lil' Bird was full of curiosity. No matter what I was doing in the yard, she was always under my feet. I had to be careful to avoid stepping on her. Lillian and I decided we needed a new barbecue grill that used charcoal, so we bought one and brought it home.

Did you know?

Crows tease other animals by biting their tails and jumping away each time the animal retaliates. They also scare other animals by making predator sounds.

I found it more convenient to try and assemble it on the sidewalk at the back of the house. When taking the grill out of the box, I was very careful not to let anything fall on the ground that she might grab up and run away with. I quickly removed the small bag of bolts and put them in my pocket. I began to assemble the grill, and Lil' Bird positioned herself right under my hands and feet. Then, I dropped a bolt. In a flash, she grabbed it and ran into the open yard, knowing what I would do. I chased her all around in order to get back that bolt! This was another game she played with me. So, to satisfy her, as always, I chased her all over the yard. There was no way I could catch her, and she knew it, but nevertheless, I gave her the pleasure of staying out of my reach. After several minutes of this, she would hide the bolt. Sitting, I would watch closely and after a minute or so, I would go pick it up. I was amazed how fast she could run, duck, and dodge my every move and avoid being caught. She had her fun! And so did I!

Another friend, Vera Taylor, came from England for a visit. I wondered how Lil' Bird would react to a completely new person. At first Lil' Bird would not allow Vera to be too close. But not many days passed, and with Vera's persistence, the gap diminished. Normally a stranger was not considered to be a friend to Lil' Bird, no matter what. If I was holding Lil' Bird or she was on my shoulder, she would huddle close to me. If the person came too close, she would give a warning by screaming in a very loud voice. That meant to get back! To my surprise, after a few days of playing with her and talking to her, Vera was able to get as close as I did. Vera could not touch her but taught her to get on a stick she held in her hand. She could then hold her at eye level on the stick and Lil' Bird seemed quite content. Vera and Lil' Bird became very good friends. She was the only person, other than Lillian, who could get near her.

Our friends would come by and we would sit in the yard together. If everyone stayed put in their chairs, Lil' Bird might come quite close, close enough that they could almost reach and touch her. She would show off for my friends by getting onto my lap, leg, shoulder or arm. Many times, she would look in my shirt pocket for a piece of paper. If she found one, she would take it out, play with it for a few seconds and stuff it back in the pocket. She might repeat this several times. She also liked to pull at my belt. Pull and tug! It would seem she was trying to destroy it. Her neck and leg muscles were much stronger than you might think. I am sure they needed to be in order for her to survive in the wild. She could dig a hole with her beak in nothing flat, especially if she found a grub or earthworm. She used her beak much like a flicker digging a hole in the ground.

CHAPTER FIFTEEN

PEPSI, ANYONE?

*What did Lil' Bird like to do with Mac's Pepsi-cola cans?

While I was drinking Pepsi-Cola from a can one day, Lil' Bird was sitting in my lap and became very anxious about what I was doing. She was watching me very intently and asking for a drink. She did not like what she tasted. What she did like, though, was the can! When I finished my drink, I raised the tab to the up position and then placed the can on the ground. She immediately jumped out of my lap, grabbed the can with the small ring, and proceeded to run. After a few minutes of this, she picked the can up by its hole and raced around the yard, again having a grand time! Later, I taught her to roll the can, pushing it with her beak on the sidewalk. She would give it a quick shove and watch it roll. If it stopped, she would rush up and give it another push. I believe she was attracted to these cans because they were shiny. Pepsi cans were her favorite toys, and we made sure there were always two or three in the yard for her.

Did you know?

Crows have an excellent memory. With humans, they can remember who treated them kindly and who posed a threat. They will communicate this information to other crows, and will harass and dive bomb those who are mean to them.

CHAPTER SIXTEEN

LIL' BIRD HELPS WITH THE CHORES

LEARNING WITH MAC: GUIDED QUESTIONS

*How did Lil' Bird help with chores in the yard?

*What was in the packet that Lil' Bird found and opened? Did she like the taste?

I was always amazed at how quickly Lil' Bird responded when challenged with something different or new, even without "coaching". Here is a good example. Our driveway is made from crushed stone. During summer months small sprigs of grass make their way through this gravel, which means of course it must be removed. Removing the small sprigs can be done by just pulling them with your fingers and then casting them aside.

One day I started pulling these sprigs while Lil' Bird watched. I watched her also, wondering what she would do. She studied my movements and my hands. Suddenly, she rushed over and with her beak, grabbed the grass. With a jerk and a snatch, she pulled it out of the driveway. From that time on whenever I reached for a sprig of grass, she reached for the same sprig and pulled it out. As long as I continued to do this, she did it. The minute I stopped, she stopped. No more grass pulling for Lil' Bird. She was much stronger than you might imagine. Most of the pulling was done with her legs. She would jerk and snatch with her neck. She did not give up if the grass happened to be tough to get out. No matter what, she would get it out. On several occasions, she pulled so hard that she fell backwards when the sprig finally came out. She seemed very pleased with her accomplishments, especially this one, because she felt she was helping me.

Shortly after she began to fly, one day I got distracted and temporarily forgot about her whereabouts. I called but did not get a response, which was unusual because she always acknowledged my call. I walked around the backyard searching, but there was no Lil' Bird to be seen or heard.

Having completed this search, I moved to the front yard calling and listening. Again, no response. I stood quietly for a moment, knowing that if she saw me, she would respond. Sure enough, I heard a familiar sound, one I had heard other times when we were playing together with a stick or rag. It was her "toiling", the sound she made when working very hard to take a stick or rag out of my hands. I quickly recognized the noise as coming from across the street. Almost immediately, I saw her sitting on the neighbor's fence with something in her mouth. I walked over to see what she was tugging and pulling at so persistently. She was a very determined little creature. I knew that she would not give up until she had completed the job. To my surprise, she had found a small packet of honey. This was the kind found in fast food restaurants, that humans often struggle with and then resort to using a knife to open. As I watched her, I knew in my heart that she would never get it open. I observed the struggle of sound and fury as she attacked this packet of honey with her feet, claws and beak. She tugged and pulled, holding it down with her feet and giving it all she had with her beak. Once she dropped it on the ground and I thought she would forget the honey and we could go home. Not on your life. She came off the fence, picked it up and flew back on the fence to continue the work at hand!

After about fifteen minutes, she finally managed to pull the packet apart and some of the honey began to ooze out. She immediately tasted it, looked at me standing there and dropped it on the ground. I knew she did not like the taste, which meant all her struggle was for naught. It seemed a shame. Lil' Bird had done all of this work with no reward, at least not to her satisfaction. I spoke to her, held out my arm for her to get on, and we made our way across the street to home. I could not help but wonder how many people had ever witnessed what I had just seen. It was a rare opportunity to see and appreciate Lil' Bird at work. Here, before my very eyes, I had seen something no one else had ever witnessed. It made me feel special in the moment.

CHAPTER SEVENTEEN — OUR BEDTIME AND MORNING ROUTINES

LEARNING WITH MAC: GUIDED QUESTIONS

*What breakfast would Mac and Lil' Bird share?

*What would Lil' Bird do with her leftover bread?

In the late afternoons I would notice that Lil' Bird would be getting tired. She would go to her house, jump on her perch and just sit there. She was ready for me to close her door, which I locked each night. As the sun set, or shortly before, she would make her way to her top roosting position. She would place herself at the door opening, so that when I opened the door, she was at my eye level and in this same spot every night. Not one night had passed that I did not go out and check on her. When I opened the door, in the darkness, she was there, and I would speak to her. She always acknowledged my presence with a low "cooing" sound. She often moved closer to me, if I was not close enough. We were usually only an inch or two apart. Sometimes I would rub her back or stroke her before closing and locking the door. She knew I was coming to see her at night and rather expected me. Her reactions convinced me beyond any doubt. This was another way she demonstrated her love. I am sure she knew all about love in her own way.

In the early morning, I could hear her calling me. From our bathroom window, she could see and hear me when I spoke to her. She acknowledged me as I spoke, by changing the tone of her call and gently flapping her wings. We understood each other. Lil' Bird knew I would be along in a few minutes with her food, as our habit was. She remained very patient until I appeared on the porch and made my way toward her house. Not so much that she was hungry, but that we were going to get together again. By now Lil' Bird was very excited, flapping her wings and jumping from one roosting bar to the next: first up and then down.

38

At this point, she would be talking a blue streak. She would be making all kinds of voice inflections, trying her best to imitate what I was saying to her; "Lil' Bird, Hello!" I wanted so much for her to talk plainly to me, but she never said any human words. She made herself known to me through her language and felt safe and secure that we understood each other. And we did. I never doubted her messages. I knew exactly what she was trying to tell me. Her actions spoke louder than words. How did I know this?

As I opened her door, she was almost always on her top roosting bar at eye level. When I spoke, she would gently touch my face with her beak. She might even rub her head against my face, all the while talking to me in her way. I would offer her my hand, and she would hop on, and we would walk to the back porch together. Sometimes she might get on my shoulder and occasionally, she would hop down on the ground, and we would walk together to the porch. By this time, she was ready for her meal. I discovered that crows meet most of their daily food requirements in the morning and she seemed hungry at that time of day.

I would bring my coffee and toast out on the porch to eat with her. Very quickly she learned to enjoy toast with jelly on it. Together we would have our meal, usually with Lil' Bird sitting on my lap. She did not like to drink coffee, but on a couple of occasions, when the coffee was warm, she would give herself a coffee bath! After I set the cup down, she would accomplish this by flipping the coffee out of the cup onto herself. It was quite humorous!

She could not eat a full slice of bread, so what was left, she buried or hid. She would hold the bread down with her foot, and tear it into smaller pieces, before putting it away for safekeeping. She seldom got to retrieve her stash because the birds and squirrels would find it first. Regardless of the outcome, she always seemed to enjoy this chore.

CHAPTER EIGHTEEN

A CLOSER LOOK AT LIL' BIRD

*What color were Lil' Bird's feathers?

*What covers Lil' Bird's ears and nasal passages?

*How many sets of eyelids did Lil' Bird have?

I really marveled at Lil' Bird's intelligence, her keen sense of hearing and her extraordinary eyesight. She was so beautiful! There is just no other word to describe her. Her feathers were black and dark blue. The blue feathers covered her back and formed row after row of scalloped patterns, all in perfect order. Her ears were covered with small downey looking feathers. The ear cavities seemed quite large for her size. They were very sensitive. She could hear noises and sounds that we cannot hear. She did not have to see a car driving into the yard or someone walking toward our backyard. She could hear all of this long before I was aware of what was going on. Lil' Bird's nasal cavities were positioned at the rear of her upper beak, again covered with small down-like feathers. When she shed these feathers, I had a good view of this part of her anatomy before they grew back in a few days.

Nasal cavities are positioned at the rear of the upper beak and are covered with small downey feathers

Ear openings are hidden beneath feathers on the side of the head

Her eyes were the most fascinating part of her body. They were quite large and sharp looking. She did not look at you straight on; it was always with one eye or the other. The eyeball did not seem to move, but she had two eye lids. One moved from back to front and the other moved from bottom to top. The first looked like a membrane, very thin, but you could not see her eyeball if it was closed. I wondered whether she could see me. I believe she could. I thought this membrane might provide protection for her eyes during flight. That is pure speculation, of course. The second lid was more like a thin skin and closed over the first lid when she slept or was resting. They were perfectly synchronized.

Did you know?

Crows aren't so much left- or right-beaked as they are left- or right-eyed. In other words, the birds are using their notable binocular vision for better monocular vision, allowing each eye to see further toward the other side of the beak.

Her mouth and beak were interesting in that she used each for a specific purpose. In addition to feeding herself, she used her mouth to keep you at bay, if she did not know you. She could, in addition to making a very loud noise, also make a hissing sound that warned, "Keep your distance!" She would not attack; she would just stay out of the way and distance herself with her warning signals.

*What were some possible dangers to Lil' Bird?

*Because he wanted what was best for Lil' Bird, what did Mac decide?

*In what ways did Lil' Bird show her love and care for Mac?

Hard cat food was now a favorite food, and Lil' Bird could easily break it up into smaller pieces with one pounding of the beak. Her beak was not a weapon. She never tried to use it on me in that way, but it did help provide for her daily food needs. She almost always used it in combination with her feet. Holding the food down with her foot and tearing it apart with her beak. It really was surprising how strong and persistent she was in getting what she wanted. By observing Lil' Bird, I learned so much about how crows survive in the wild. They are tough little creatures with instincts that baffle man, even today. It is strange; man could not survive their conditions nor could crows, if they had their choice, survive under man's conditions. They each need their freedom to act on their own. I discovered this later on.

I was concerned and worried a great deal about Lil' Bird not being able to fly. I wondered if I had done something to cause her to not want to fly or if she had decided on her own that she would forget about flying and remain with us. I continuously feared for her safety when one of us was not around. Now she was quite tame, as we walked together, but sometimes she would get out into the street, where cars were coming and going. She did not fear cars. She was accustomed to riding in cars and getting in and out of them, so she saw no danger. If she wandered off into the street, I would pick her up and bring her back into the yard. I wanted so badly for her to fly, for her own safety. Yet, I felt if she did ever learn to fly, she would soon leave. I knew I would have to give her up to her wild instincts. It was bound to happen. I did not want to see Lil' Bird get hit by an automobile.

It was at this point I determined, as much as we had grown together and loved each other, that I would prefer to see her leave. I had now brought myself around to the idea that, even if she left, she would come back to see us later. Several people shared that view with me. Providing that nothing tragic happened to her, I believed she would come back.

No one could fully understand my feelings for Lil' Bird or how she felt towards me. How could such closeness develop between a little wild crow and an old man. What pleasure, what joy, what love! She won my heart, and I felt deeply for her. Her actions and her antics were more than proof to me that our feelings were mutual. Time and time again, too numerous to remember, she touched me on the face or cuddled close to me to rest, completely trusting me with her life. She would eat from my hand and even gently take a piece of cookie from my mouth, which again was an expression of utter and complete trust. She trusted me as we walked together, staying close by, knowing I would protect her if danger appeared on the scene. She never got too far out of my sight and if I called her, she would respond to my call. Our kitchen door that opened onto the porch, was always open, as was the door that lead to the basement. If she was in the basement and I called for her to come, she would hop up the steps into the kitchen. There were times I would turn around and there she would be on the floor, looking up and calling in her way, to let me know she was there, probably wanting something to eat. By now, she could really make her way up and down stairs without any trouble. She was a smart little cookie, and she knew it. She would respond to my communications in her own language, in a way that I could understand.

CHAPTER TWENTY

LIL' BIRD'S NEW FOUND ADVENTURE: FLYING

LEARNING WITH MAC: GUIDED QUESTIONS

*What happened shortly before Lil' Bird flew for the first time?

*How did Lil' Bird's behavior change once she learned to fly?

In late summer I noticed Lil' Bird was losing some of her feathers. I found several in her house and upon examination I discovered they were the ones that we had clipped when we first found her. I did not realize until then that the feathers had grown in width only, that the length had remained about the same. This was true of the wing, as well as the tail feathers, and having observed other wild crows in our yard or flying over our house, I knew her wing and tail feathers were not nearly long enough for her to fly. Almost every day another feather or two fell out, or she pulled them out. I could also see new feathers coming in to replace the old ones. In two or three weeks she had a complete set of both tail and wing feathers. I could hardly believe that this happened so quickly. I was not familiar with the molting process of crows, but molt they did, and in short order.

Finally, one day when I came home, Lillian met me at the door with the news that Lil' Bird had made her first flight around the yard.

It was only a short distance, but nevertheless she had managed to fly!

After a day or so of this, she really caught on and she was now flying everywhere. She would take two or three laps around the house and then return to the backyard. Lil' Bird was so proud of her new accomplishment. When I sat in my chair, she would fly over to me, perching herself on the arm of the chair or on my shoulder. In her own way, she would tell me of her newfound adventure. No longer was she dependent on me to pick her up or offer her my arm to transport her from place to place. She did not have to walk, now that she could fly! Having now taken to the air, she quickly forgot most of her dependency on me and truly discovered her freedom. She never ventured very far from her surroundings, but would fly up to the top of the large oak tree in our backyard or the roof of our house or garage. She always remained in calling distance.

If I left her in the yard alone, she might fly to some place I could not see her; however if I called, she would answer. I could easily distinguish her sound from the other crows in the area or the ones flying overhead. If I was able to see her, when I called, she not only responded, but would also flap her wings as she had always done, almost from the beginning. She never failed to do this. Most of the time she would come to me on my first call. She would land within five or six feet, directly in front of me and look up as if to say, "How did you like that landing?"

Did you know?

Feathers are made of keratin, a protein similar to human hair and nails, and they can't heal themselves when damaged. Molting replaces damaged or worn feathers with new ones, which helps birds fly efficiently, regulate their temperature, and protect themselves.

CHAPTER TWENTY ONE

THE CALLING OF THE CROWS

LEARNING WITH MAC: GUIDED QUESTIONS

*What would Lil' Bird do if Mac did not answer her call?

*Once Lil' Bird could fly, how did her relationship and interaction with other crows change?

Sometimes I would walk out into the backyard and not call, but just stand quietly. If Lil' Bird saw me, she would call me. If I did not answer, in a matter of seconds, I would feel a "swish" behind my back and again she would be at my feet looking up at me. She always approached me from the rear, her wings almost touching me as she went by. She never approached from the front. I thought that was very unusual and have no idea why she did it this way. When sitting on the porch swing, she would come from behind and land on the swing beside me or on the floor in front of me. She liked the porch railing as a place to rest. When I was inside, she would sit on the railing and call for me to come. She also learned quickly to sit on the windowsill and look at me through the window. She demanded attention and companionship and had figured out a way to get this done. I gave her all the attention I could, for hours upon hours. For this I was richly rewarded. Even though she was a wild creature, Lil' Bird entertained me, and all those around her, in ways that were ever new and surprising. Twice while standing in the open yard, she tried to land on top of my head. Since I had no hat on, she would slide off my head and onto my shoulders. She gave me the feeling that she was having fun at my expense. She had learned she would never accomplish the feat of landing on my head, so she just continued to land in front of me.

I ceased to worry about her after she learned to fly. Being able to fly protected Lil' Bird in many ways and provided me with relief from my concerns. But now my concerns shifted to something else.

Almost from the day we first had Lil' Bird with us, other crows would fly by and call from the nearby trees. I am sure she was originally part of a family group, the crows who nested in the pine tree. While young, she did not acknowledge them in any way. She might glance in their direction as they flew by, but made no noise. She paid more attention to airplanes passing overhead. She watched them carefully as they crossed over our house, looking as if she knew exactly what they were.

As Lil' Bird grew older, I noticed she began to pay more attention and listen to the family of crows. I am sure this group of crows communicated with and understood each other. One day, two of Lil' Bird's friends came down to the ground and they played together for several minutes. This was something I thought would never happen. However, they came and went on occasion. Their visits were getting longer and longer. By now, I was firmly convinced that these were her family members. They were coming more frequently, especially in the early morning hours. They would fly around and call out loudly. They seemed to get louder each day. Lil' Bird watched and listened but made no attempt to join them. She did not give me any reason to think that someday, she might do just that. Fall was approaching. The weather was changing and now my attention focused on how I would provide for her during the cold winter months.

Lil' Bird loved her home, and after a long and tiring day, she would come to me and together we would go to her house. There, I would feed her and bed her down for the night. If for some reason, I did not come in time to take her to her house, she would go in, hop on her perch and wait for me to come with her food. She did not eat much late in the day. We would always visit for a while before I closed and locked her door. I am sure she knew that the door was locked to keep her safe and sound. It occurred to me that to further protect her from the wind, rain and cold winter winds, we would need to modify her house by wrapping it in heavy plastic and installing a small electric heater to keep her warm. I even considered arranging a place for her in our basement but felt she would be less confused in her house. Finally, I decided to use both. For severe cold conditions, she would be in the basement and out in her place on the other days. In the meantime, I had read several short articles about crows, some of their habits, and how they survived in cold conditions. They migrated for short distances, mainly to heavy wooded areas with good winter-feeding grounds. I read that in extremely wintery conditions, they huddled close and that the warmth of the group helped to keep them very comfortable, even in the worst possible conditions. They are described as very hardy and tough. Still, I could not help but be concerned about Lil' Bird. She was my full responsibility, and nothing was going to happen to her, as long as I had her in my charge. I would see to that.

Now with each passing day, her friends returned, more insistent with their calls. They were flying in every direction and making very loud noises, trying to entice her to come with them. She paid more attention to them now. Lil' Bird was watching them very carefully, trying to determine what she must do. Of course, at the time I did not place much stock in what was taking place, but now as I review the past, the whole story makes sense to me.

She was enticed to leave and go with them. It was time to seek the winter haven and feeding grounds. I know during those days, she was torn between staying with us or leaving with them. Her wild instincts were taking over and she would be joining her crow family. Her decision was best. She may not have survived on her own, being alone without the companionship of her own kind. In a family situation, secure in each other and protected, they could survive in the wild conditions, which she now faced.

CHAPTER TWENTY-TWO

AND NOW WE SAY GOODBYE

LEARNING WITH MAC: GUIDED QUESTIONS

*How did Lil' Bird say goodbye?

*How did Mac feel when Lil' Bird left?

This is what happened on the last morning we were together. As usual, she called me early in the morning. I answered her from my bathroom window. She acknowledged my response, gently flapping her wings and took her position on her lower perch. I made our piece of toast with jelly before going out to her house. As I was going toward her house, her crow friends gathered again and began making their usual loud noises and calls. There were about eight in the group that morning, flying wildly overhead, all trying to fly in different patterns. I paid little attention, but noticed that Lil' Bird was watching what was going on, rather intently.

 I opened the door. She was sitting on her upper perch, now at eye level with me. She spoke as she always did, rushed over, put her beak against my face, and jumped on my shoulder. She placed her head against my face, then jumped on top of the door to her house. I walked toward the house where we usually went to have our breakfast together and she flew onto the porch railing. She beat me there and was waiting. As Lil' Bird sat on the railing, I offered her some toast and she took a small piece and looked at me rather puzzled. The crows flying overhead were now screaming very loudly, as she watched. She then took another small piece of toast. She did not eat it, but stuffed it in a small crack in the railing. She then gave me a long parting look, as if to say, "I must go now. Thank you for taking care of me. I love you." and with that, in a flash, she joined her family, and they left together.

I thought my heart would almost burst. I could hardly contain myself as the tears came. I let them come, and felt a deep sense of emptiness. Some part of me was gone. I wanted to call her, but I did not, because I knew she would not come back. I also knew it was best for her to go. That knowledge did not make it any easier, though. I just stood in silence and our happy times together all flashed before me. My eyes began to fill with tears again. It was just too much. After five months together, would it end this way? I sat on the back porch steps and once again the tears came. I knew she was gone out of my life, forever, and that our relationship would now be a memory.

That last morning did tell me a great deal about Lil' Bird, the closeness of our relationship and how much we loved each other. How do I know this? When I opened her door that morning, she could have flown out, joined the other birds and gone on her way. She did not do that, and her actions were quite clear. She would not leave me without saying goodbye, in her way. She stayed until the very last second before leaving. I am convinced that she saved those last few minutes for us to be together.

Even now, I am continually looking for her. When I hear a crow call, I wonder if it is her. I find myself worrying about her whereabouts and whether she is getting plenty to eat. I hope she is handling the cold weather all right and that she is safe with her own family. I do include her in my prayers.

I long for her to return in the Spring. Some say she will. What a thrill it would be for that to happen!

This same crow family has nested for two or three years in our neighbor's yard, and it fills my heart with hope, that maybe,

just maybe,

       my Lil' Bird
          will come back.

               The End

MAC AND LIL'BIRD EPILOGUE

I am a Christian. I believe the Lord knows our hearts and minds as no one else. He knew spending time with Lil' Bird would please me and most of all He knew it would be an unforgettable experience that would be a part of me for the remaining days of my life. Opportunities come to us more often than we think or even see. Some we brush aside, and then there are those that we cannot ignore. The "still, small voice" speaks, and we listen. Such was my case.

Some two or three weeks after Lil' Bird had gone, I would wake up and recount our times together. Over and over again these memories were replayed, much like a movie. This happened night after night. Eventually I would go back to sleep, but the following night it would happen again. This continued for several weeks.

Finally one night, the message came. I sensed I was supposed to make a record of this experience and share it with others. Maybe my children and grandchildren. It was not my purpose to write anything. I only wanted to preserve in a simple way my unique experience having Lil' Bird as part of my life. Since I was not a writer, I wondered how I was supposed to do this. Again an answer came…write the facts down as they happened. From this information, someone could then come up with an interesting story.

As soon as I had completed recording all the events, my wakeful and restless nights ceased. Yes, this seems mystifying, and so it was. I have no explanation except to say this urgency, this need to do something, was undeniable.

And so my story ends here of a loving and endearing relationship that enriched my life. It has been said that the simple and unexpected pleasures and experiences often become our most precious moments and remembrances. Lest we forget, God gave us His Word and I believe the promises there in. All of the victories and goodness in my life have come from our heavenly Father. I give Him the credit, glory and honor.

STAFFORD L. BOLTON (MAC)

A MESSAGE FROM MAC

THE FOLLOWING WAS ORIGINALLY A MESSAGE FOR MAC'S WIFE, LILLIAN, HIS CHILDREN, AND GRANDCHILDREN. MAC, WHO THE FAMILY LOVINGLY REFERRED TO AS DADDY AND GRAN, WAS A PILLAR OF INTEGRITY AND GODLY WISDOM. FOR THIS REASON, THE BOLTON FAMILY WISHES TO SHARE HIS FINAL THOUGHTS AND ENCOURAGEMENT WITH YOU, THE READERS OF THE STORY HE HOPED MIGHT BE WRITTEN SOMEDAY ABOUT HIS TIME WITH LIL' BIRD.

Lil' Bird came to us in a very special way for a special visit. Who would have ever guessed how very much the events that followed and recorded here would mean to us and to those who witnessed her presence and saw first-hand the story being shared here. One thing stands out above all else and is confirmed by this experience. As the scriptures have taught us, God created all things out of love, which is the key ingredient of His creation.

Lil' Bird loved us - of this I am sure. The key ingredient was there - evident in all of her actions and shown many times and in numerous ways. The joy and pleasure we shared together with her was another way God was sharing His love for and with us. Imagine God demonstrating His love for us through a little, black crow! Amazing! Unbelievable!! But that is exactly what He did!

Now a final message to my children and grandchildren. Life is full of little surprises and extra pleasures. They are given to you to enjoy. Be watchful and alert and always ready to take advantage of these "specials." Remember they were designed for you by the ONE who knows you best and what makes you happy. This was one of my "specials," as it came to me late in my life. My hope is having shared it in this way, you may come to love, enjoy, and appreciate my little friend and remember her as your friend, too!

all my love
mac.

A FAMILY AFFAIR
BRINGING MAC'S STORY TO PRINT

Elijah Walls worked hard on researching most of the "Did You Know" facts that are found throughout the story.

Emerson Walls worked diligently on the "How to Draw a Crow" illustrations.

Tracey Walls helped coordinate the efforts of her family and worked with Suminski Family Books to get the book to print.

Tracey Walls and family pictured on the left.

The Bolton Family
Pictured in front: Mac and Lillian
Back row: Stafford, Beverly, Susan, and Marshall (Monk)

Mac and Lillian

Bolton Family
Recipes

Bev's Chocolate Sauce

Ingredients:

1 cup sugar

1/2 cup cocoa

2 tbsp. flour

¼ tsp. salt

1 cup boiling water

1 tbsp. butter

½ tsp. vanilla

Blend sugar, cocoa, flour, and salt. Add boiling water and butter. Cook until thick, stirring constantly. Remove from heat and add vanilla. Serve hot over ice cream. May be stored in your refrigerator and reheated as needed.

Bev's Pimento Cheese

Ingredients:

2 - 8 oz. blocks Cabot Seriously Sharp cheddar cheese finely grated

1 - 4 oz. jar diced pimentos

1 cup Miracle Whip (to spreadable consistency)

In a bowl, add grated cheese and empty contents of the jar of pimentos, including liquid. Stir mixture to distribute pimentos. Add Miracle Whip to spreadable consistency. Delicious on bread or crackers.

Mother's Fruit Cobbler

Ingredients:

1 cup sugar

1 cup flour

1 cup milk

1 stick butter

3 tsp. baking powder

Fruit of choice (2 cans)

Heat oven to 375°. Mix sugar, flour, milk, and baking powder. Melt butter in pan (9 x 13). Pour batter over melted butter. Drop spoons of fruit over batter. Sprinkle sugar over batter. Bake about 40 min. or until batter is golden brown.

Chicken Casserole

Ingredients:

4 chicken breasts

1 can cream of celery soup

¾ can chicken broth

½ bag Pepperidge Farm Stuffing Mix - herb

1 stick butter

Cook chicken until tender; pull off bone; place in greased casserole dish. Mix soup and broth and pour over chicken. Then add dressing mix; dribble 1 stick butter over this. Bake at 325° for 25 min.

Aunt Lila's Corn Pudding

Ingredients:
1 egg
½ tsp. salt
1 tbsp. sugar
1 ½ tbs. flour or corn starch
1 cup milk
1 can cream style corn
1 small piece of butter
½ tsp. vanilla

Beat egg. Mix flour, salt, sugar together and stir into egg. Add milk, corn, butter, and vanilla. Cook 20 to 25 minutes in not too hot oven - about 300°. Do not let boil.

Meet the Illustrator
Isabella Ross Unrein

Isabella is a young, home-schooled, professional artist from Eastern North Carolina. She focuses on painting and sketching, inspired by the beauty of nature, particularly local wildlife and landscapes. She has done watercolor paintings for illustrations, nature prints, greeting cards, and custom pet portraits. Isabella also enjoys spending time in nature, listening to and making music, good food, and spending time with friends and family.

You can contact her at isabella@unrein.life

You can check out her website,
https://www.unrein.life/isabella.html

MAC AND LIL' BIRD WORD SEARCH

```
T F P W J F P G I B W P A O T
R E Q H J N E R U K X S W A R
C I R P G H X A X C F H I B O
M N L R R I C C T K Y Y N B U
O S U F I E N M O H C N G R T
L T Z S L T D C A O E L S Y I
T I Y Q C A O A U C P R R X N
I N O U U T P R T B X K S N E
N C Z I R K W P Y O A X Y E E
G T J R I J U C I B R T E S L
S T G R O F L B Y N M S I T J
G B Q E S Z X H D X G Z D O D
B K J L I N G C I V U C V X N
H M S B T U Y X O F L Y I N G
T J C A Y C X H C R O P A P B
```

INCUBATION	CURIOSITY	PREDATORS
FEATHERS	TERRITORY	INSTINCT
FLAPPING	FLYING	ROUTINE
COOP	MOLTING	CROP
SQUIRREL	WINGS	NEST

The Digestive Sytems of Birds

Here is a list of the digestive parts of birds and their definitions.

Bills:
Bills come in all different sizes and shapes and are used for scooping, pecking, tearing and generally picking up the bird's food.

Mouth:
The bird's mouth is the opening where the digestive process starts.

Tongue:
The tongue is used to direct the food item down the digestive tract and sometimes to help hold onto a wiggling worm or other insect.

Pharynx:
The pharynx (FAIR – ingx) is the part between the mouth and esophagus that helps the bird swallow the food item.

Esophagus:
The esophagus is the tube leading down from the pharynx to the crop.

Crop:
The crop is like a "doggy bag" when the bird eats. Many birds eat as much as possible when the opportunity for feeding presents itself. This food can't possibly be digested this quick. The crop enables the bird to fill up and then the bird can do the digesting later when it has time to rest and avoid predators that may be lurking nearby while the bird is in the act of eating.

Proventriculus:

The proventriculus is the first part of the bird's two-chambered stomach. The proventriculus secretes an acid used for breaking down food, and is best developed in birds that swallow entire fish or other animals containing bones which must be digested.

Gizzard:

The gizzard is the second chamber of the stomach and it consists of very tough muscles. These muscles are used to grind and digest various types of foods. The muscles don't do this process alone. Many birds pick up small pebbles, sand or grit while they are eating and these items end up in the gizzard. The gizzard then uses these grit-like items to help pulverize the food items to aid in digestion. Different bird species eat different food items and their gizzards are designed to work specifically on the types of food that they eat.

Small Intestines:

The intestines are where the nutrients from the food are absorbed and the waste products are sent further on through the digestive system. This is very similar to the human intestine function. Birds that eat easily digestible foods like fruit, flesh and insects have short lengths of intestines and those that eat seeds, plants and fish need longer intestines so that the food items have enough time for the nutrients to be absorbed.

Caeca:

The word caeca (SEE-kah) is plural for caecum (SEE-kum) because birds usually have two of them. The function of the caeca is to aid in the absorption of water and proteins, and the microbial decomposition of fiber.

Rectum:

The rectum is the end part of the intestine and no digestion or absorption of food takes place here.

Cloaca:

The cloaca (klo-A-ka) is the end of the digestive tract where waste from the digestive and urinary tract accumulate before being dumped. Many times the waste is a white liquid with a dark center. Uric acid is a by-product of the bird's digestive system.

Breaking down the parts into three categories may make it easier to remember the parts and definitions. See what you can remember by playing the matching game on the next page.

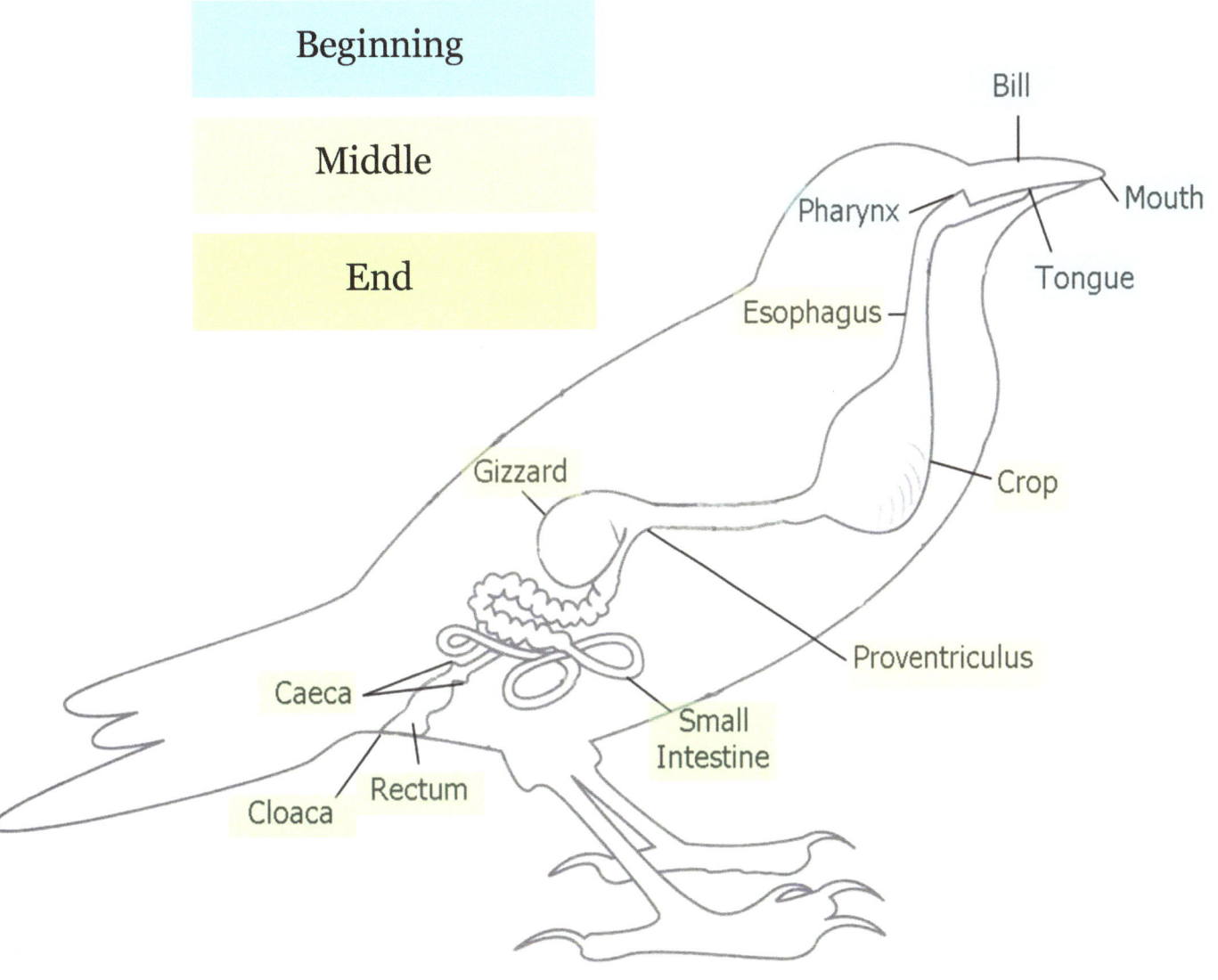

Beginning

Middle

End

Bill

Mouth

Pharynx

Tongue

Esophagus

Gizzard

Crop

Proventriculus

Caeca

Small Intestine

Rectum

Cloaca

BIRD DIGESTIVE SYSTEM MATCHING GAME

Match the word on the left with the definition on the right.

Bill	the end of the digestive tract where waste from the digestive and urinary tract accumulate before being dumped
Caeca	the first part of the bird's two-chambered stomach
Cloaca	used for scooping, pecking, tearing and generally picking up the bird's food
Crop	aids in the absorption of water and proteins, and the microbial decomposition of fiber
Esophagus	second chamber of the stomach consists of very tough muscles used to grind and digest various types of foods
Gizzard	part between the mouth and esophagus that helps the bird swallow the food item
Mouth	the end part of the intestine
Pharynx	like a "doggy bag" when the bird eats
Proventriculus	used to direct the food item down the digestive tract
Rectum	where the nutrients from the food are absorbed and the waste products are sent further on through the digestive system
Small Intestine	the tube leading down from the pharynx to the crop
Tongue	the opening where the digestive process starts

Answers can be found on the Answer page

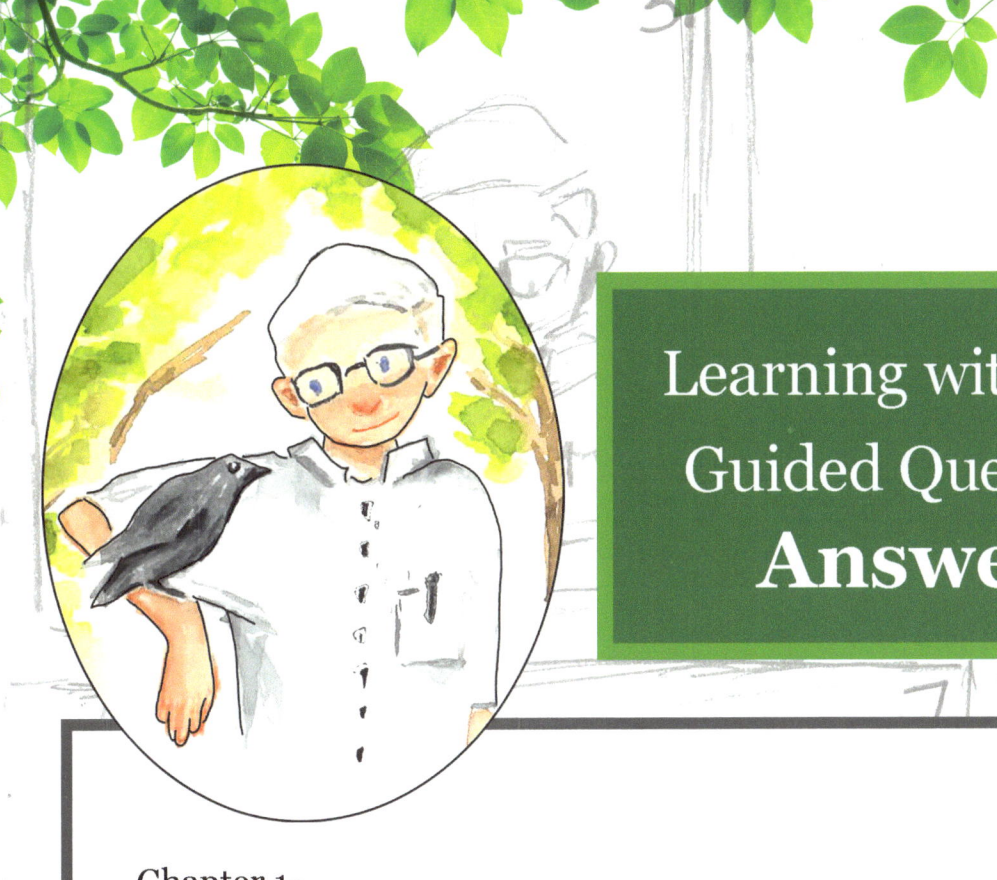

Learning with Mac: Guided Questions
Answers

Chapter 1-

What had Mac heard about crows?

That they could be taught to talk by imitating the human voice

Chapter 2-

What were some of the jobs in the crow family?

Gather food, care for the nest, guard the surrounding area, sound an alarm when there was danger, drive away intruders

What is the incubation period for crow eggs?

28 days

Chapter 3-

How did the adult crows react to Mac approaching Lil' Bird?

They circled overhead, screeching loudly.

How did Lil' Bird react to Mac trying to pick her up?

She jumped out of the holly tree and ran a short distance away from him.

Chapter 4-

Why were Lil' Bird's wings clipped?

They seemed uneven and they felt they might care for her better if she did not fly until she had gotten older and larger.

What was Lil' Bird's preferred food?

Small balls of dampened cornmeal and small pieces of white bread soaked in water

Chapter 5-

How did Lil' Bird let people know if they had gotten too close to her?

She made a specific noise that let everyone know that she was not happy.

How did Lil' Bird show Mac that she was listening when he spoke to her?

She would cock her head sideways and look intently at him..

What kinds of things did Lil' Bird like to play with?

Anything that was shiny or reflected light

Chapter 6-

How did Lil' Bird greet Mac in the mornings?

She would gently flap her wings.

When Mac became concerned about Lil' Bird's quarters in the garage, where did he move her?

To the basement of their home

Chapter 7-

Why did Lil' Bird pretend to have a broken wing?

Both male and female crows sometimes pretend to have injured wings in order to lead predators away from their young.

Did Lil' Bird ever sit on Lillian's arm?

Yes, but only reluctantly once or twice.

Chapter 8-

What did Lil' Bird do if another bird got into her new house?

She would hurry from wherever she was and drive them out.

What part of Lil' Bird's body was not growing with the rest of her? Why was this a problem?

Her feathers, wings, and tail were not growing well. It might have meant she would never be able to fly.

Chapter 9-

What would Lil' Bird do to Mac's clothing?

Try to pull off his buttons, pull at any loose strings, untie his shoes

What makes crows so clumsy when they walk?

Their large feet

Describe Lil' Bird's behavior when she was trying to talk to Mac.

She would lower her head to her breast, then slowly raise it making guttural, throaty sounds

Chapter 10-

How did Lil' Bird feel about her bathtub and bath time?

She loved it and would often take two or three baths a day.

How long did it take for Lil' Bird to preen her feathers after bath time?

Thirty to forty-five minutes

What did Mac use to protect his arm from Lil' Bird's claws?

A heavy stocking

Chapter 11-

If Lil' Bird noticed Mac going to his car, how did she respond?

She would fly from wherever she was and land on the hood of the car. She would not move unless she was allowed to get into the car and go with him.

Why did visitors to the Bolton home have to be careful about closing their car doors?

Lil' Bird would climb into their car.

Chapter 12-

How would Lil' Bird eat her cookies and peanut butter crackers?

She would take them to the back porch, smash them with her beak, and eat them.

Where did Lil' Bird store food?

A little pouch in her throat called a "crop.

What were some of the places that Lil' Bird would try to hide her food?

Under leaves or sticks, in Mac's shoes, shirt pocket, and the creases of his clothes

Chapter 13-

What did Lil' Bird leave in her food dish for Mac?

Nails and staples that had been left in the yard from building her house

How did Lil' Bird let Mac know she was ready to play?

She would find a stick and bring it to him.

Chapter 14-

What did Lil' Bird do when the squirrel tried to bump her?

She jumped straight up in the air and the squirrel ran underneath her.

Chapter 14 (con't)-

What mischief did Lil' Bird make when Mac was trying to assemble his new grill?

She grabbed a bolt he dropped on the ground and ran away with it so that he would chase her. She thought it was a game.

What special visitor became friends with Lil' Bird?

Vera Taylor from England (or as Lillian always introduced her, "Vera...of England!")

Chapter 15-

What did Lil' Bird like to do with Mac's Pepsi-cola cans?

Play with them

Chapter 16-

How did Lil' Bird help with chores in the yard?

Pulling grass out of the driveway

What was in the packet that Lil' Bird found and opened? Did she like the taste?

Honey, no

Chapter 17-

What breakfast would Mac and Lil' Bird share?

Jelly toast and coffee. Lil' Bird wouldn't drink the coffee, but sometimes she would take a "coffee bath."

What would Lil' Bird do with her leftover bread?

She would tear it into smaller pieces and then bury or hide it.

Chapter 18-

What color were Lil' Bird's feathers?

Black and dark blue

What covers Lil' Bird's ears and nasal passages?

small downey looking feathers

How many sets of eyelids did Lil' Bird have?

Two, one set closed from top to bottom and the other closed from back to front.

Chapter 19-

What were some possible dangers to Lil' Bird?

She could not fly. She was not afraid of cars, so she would often wander into the street.

Because he wanted what was best for Lil' Bird, what did Mac decide?

He decided that it would be best for her to leave and live in the wild.

Chapter 19 (con't)-

In what ways did Lil' Bird show her love and care for Mac?

She touched him on the face and cuddled close with him to rest. She would eat from his hand and take a cookie from his mouth. She always stayed close to him and came quickly if he called her.

Chapter 20-

What happened shortly before Lil' Bird flew for the first time?

She molted, she her old feathers and grew new ones.

How did Lil' Bird's behavior change once she learned to fly?

She ventured a bit farther away from the house and Mac than she had before.

Chapter 21-

What would Lil' Bird do if Mac did not answer her call?

She would fly behind his back and land at his feet to get his attention.

Once Lil' Bird could fly, how did her relationship and interaction with other crows change?

She paid more attention to them. Sometimes some of the crows would come onto the ground and spend time with her.

Chapter 22-

How did Lil' Bird say goodbye?

She took a piece of toast, stuffed it in a crack in the porch railing, stared at Mac, and then flew away with her family.

How did Mac feel when Lil' Bird left?

He was sad, but knew it was best for her to go and be with her family.

MAC AND LIL' BIRD WORD SEARCH

ANSWER PAGE

BIRD DIGESTIVE SYSTEM MATCHING GAME

Bill

Caeca

Cloaca

Crop

Esophagus

Gizzard

Mouth

Pharynx

Proventriculus

Rectum

Small Intestine

Tongue

the end of the digestive tract where waste from the digestive and urinary tract accumulate before being dumped

the first part of the bird's two-chambered stomach

used for scooping, pecking, tearing and generally picking up the bird's food

aids in the absorption of water and proteins, and the microbial decomposition of fiber

second chamber of the stomach consists of very tough muscles used to grind and digest various types of foods

part between the mouth and esophagus that helps the bird swallow the food item

the end part of the intestine

like a "doggy bag" when the bird eats

used to direct the food item down the digestive tract

where the nutrients from the food are absorbed and the waste products are sent further on through the digestive system

the tube leading down from the pharynx to the crop

the opening where the digestive process starts

Suminski Family Books

FAITH, FAMILY, DILIGENCE, AND LOVE

Find more read aloud stories for the whole family to enjoy at:

www.suminskifamilybooks.com